# ENJOY PLAYING THE GUITAR
## BOOK 2

## Quick Reference

Use this page to check notes, time signatures etc., that have been covered in *Enjoy Playing the Guitar Book 1*.

### Natural Notes

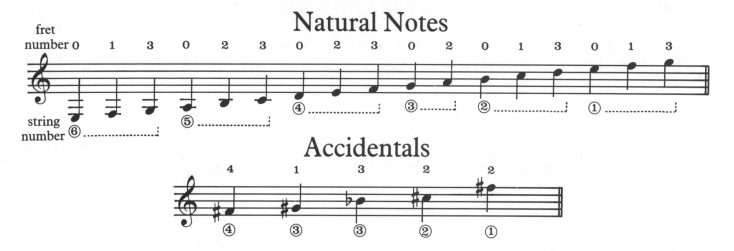

### Accidentals

## Time Signatures

$\frac{4}{4}$ = Four crotchet beats to a bar

$\frac{3}{4}$ = Three crotchet beats to a bar

$\frac{6}{4}$ = Six crotchet beats to a bar

$\frac{6}{8}$ = Six quaver beats to a bar

## Terms and Signs

$f$ = loud    $mf$ = moderately loud

$mp$ = moderately soft    $p$ = soft    $pp$ = very soft

rall. = getting slower    Adagio = slow

Andante = walking pace

Allegro = fast and lively

## Keys used in Book 1

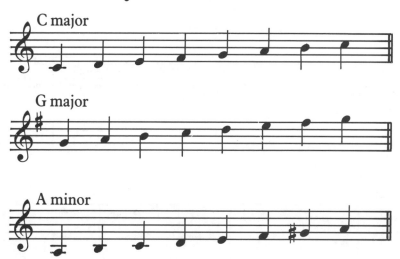

C major

G major

A minor

© Oxford University Press 1990    Printed in Great Britain
OXFORD UNIVERSITY PRESS, MUSIC DEPARTMENT, GREAT CLARENDON STREET, OXFORD OX2 6DP

# Introducing Semiquavers

This note with two tails is called a semiquaver.
It is worth half a quaver ( ♪ ) or a quarter of a crotchet ( ♩ )
When written in groups of two or more the tails are usually joined up …

Exercise 1

Exercise 2

2/4 Two crotchet beats in a bar.

## Drunken Sailor

English traditional

## Aria

Duet

Telemann
(1681–1767)

G.1

G.2

# Dance of the Fishermen

Debbie Cracknell

# Rocking Carol

Czech traditional

Duet

**Tranquillo***

G.1

G.2

*Tranquillo* = calmly, gently
*rit.* = hold back

**4**

In this early dance tune by Tylman Susato use a **ponticello** (ponti.) effect at the repeats. This is produced by moving the right hand nearer the bridge. For a simpler version, play it as a duet, with a melody line and a bass line.

## Ronde

Susato
(16th-century)

This solo is one of many pieces composed by Matteo Carcassi, an Italian composer and guitarist.

## Allegretto

Carcassi
(1792–1853)

$f$ (repeat $mp$)

*Fine*

$mp$

*D.C. al Fine*

*cresc.**

$f$

\* *cresc.* = getting gradually louder

# Two New Accidentals

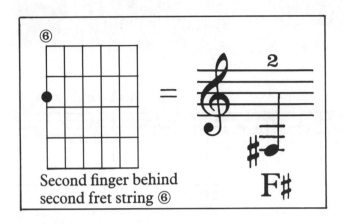
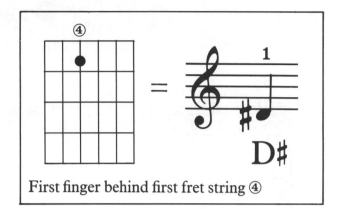

E minor scale

After practising the scale (remember the F♯ in the key signature applies to all F's, even F on string ⑥) try 'Gondola Waltz'. In 'Gondola Waltz' bring out the melody in the bass and play the chords quietly as an accompaniment.

# Gondola Waltz

Debbie Cracknell

# Boogie March

Debbie Cracknell

\* **Moderato** = at a moderate pace

# Romantic Memories

Debbie Cracknell

# Triplets

Triplets are notes grouped in threes with the figure *3* against them which indicates that there are three notes played in the time of two − i.e. triplet quavers are each worth one third of a crotchet.

**Exercise using triplets**

Count 1  2  3 4  1  2  3  4

**F major scale in triplets**

Take note of the new key signature. In F major all the B's are played flat. Remember, B♭ is found on string ③ fret 3.

Count 1  2  3  4  *simile**

\* = continue in triplets

**Tricky rhythm scale**

Count 1  2  3  4

A Tango is a dance from South America which uses the rhythm

# Tango in Thirds

Debbie Cracknell

Duet

G.1

G.2

# One new Accidental

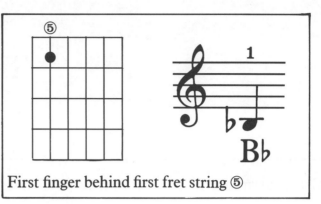

First finger behind first fret string ⑤

In 'Autumn Mists' the arpeggio accompaniment is written in triplets.
**repeat tasto** = move the right hand nearer the fretboard to produce a softer, more mellow tone.

## Autumn Mists

Debbie Cracknell

\* **a tempo** = in time

# Test

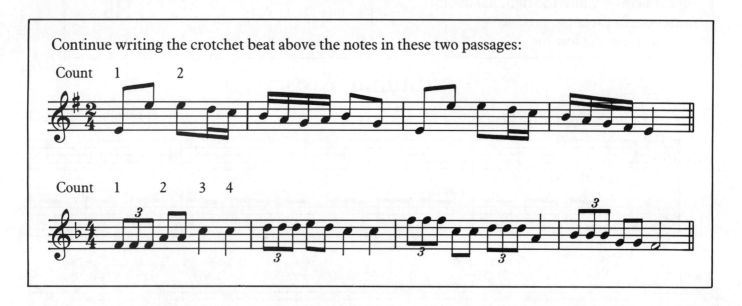

Continue writing the crotchet beat above the notes in these two passages:

Count    1        2

Count    1        2        3        4

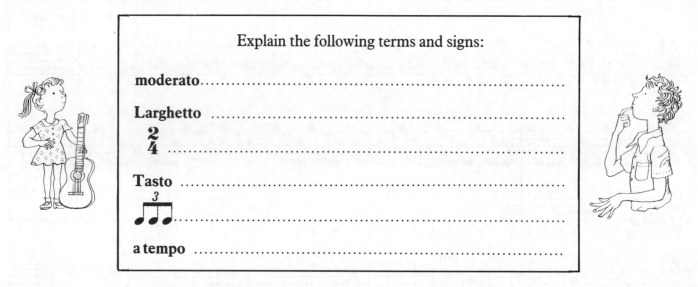

Explain the following terms and signs:

**moderato**...........................................................................

**Larghetto** ........................................................................

**2/4** ..................................................................................

**Tasto** ..............................................................................

........................................................................................

**a tempo** .........................................................................

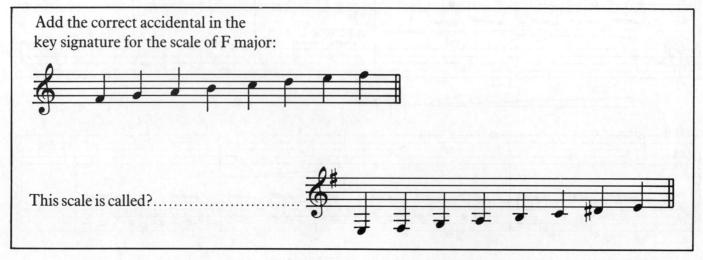

Add the correct accidental in the
key signature for the scale of F major:

This scale is called?..........................

# The Second Position

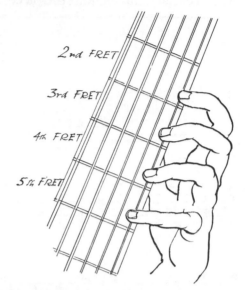

When playing in the second position (indicated by II above the music) move your hand up the fingerboard so that —

finger 1 plays notes on the 2nd fret
finger 2 plays notes on the 3rd fret
finger 3 plays notes on the 4th fret
finger 4 plays notes on the 5th fret

Make sure your thumb moves up the back of the neck until it is level with the third fret. Do not 'leave it behind'.

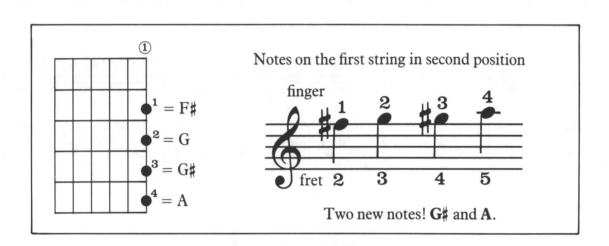

Notes on the first string in second position

Two new notes! **G♯** and **A**.

Exercise in second position

In 'Hoe-Down', Guitar 1 is played in second position. Note the new key signature — both F and C are sharp throughout the piece. This new key is called D major.

# Hoe-Down

Debbie Cracknell

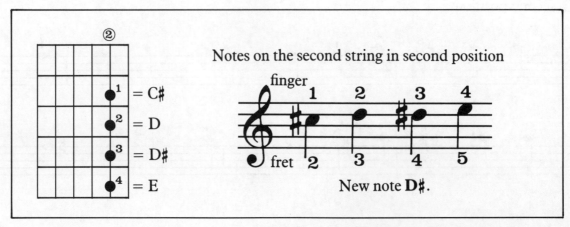

Notes on the second string in second position

New note **D♯**.

Exercise in D major

## The Sinkapace Galliard

Melody from
'William Ballet's Lute Book' (1580)

repeat ponti.

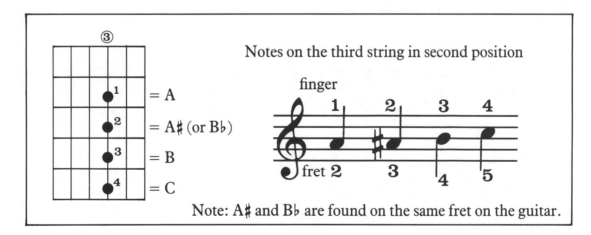

Notes on the third string in second position

③
= A
= A♯ (or B♭)
= B
= C

Note: A♯ and B♭ are found on the same fret on the guitar.

## Melody

Debbie Cracknell

# The Minstrels

**Allegretto** (fairly fast)

Debbie Cracknell

* If the E was taken here (bar 6 of 'The Minstrels') with a 4th finger on the 2nd string, there would be a hiccup as you jumped to the 4th finger A on the first string, therefore take an open E in this bar. There will be many occasions when you have to decide whether to use an open E or a fingered E. Listen to the difference in sound between both E's. Which has a warmer tone?

# Rondo

Carulli
(1770–1841)

**Allegretto**

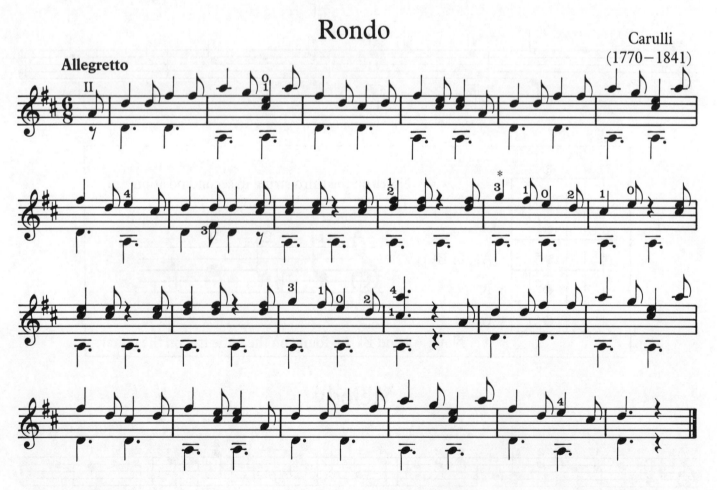

* The third finger for G here gives a smoother change from the chord.

This new key of A major has three notes sharpened in the key signature.
F, C, and G are all sharp.

Scale of A major

##Ländler
(A German Dance)

Debbie Cracknell

*mf* (repeat *p*)

*mf* (repeat *p*)

*mf* (repeat *p*)

(last time) ——— *f*

Two-note exercise

Practise this exercise
before trying 'Sweet Potato'.

In 'Sweet Potato' practise clapping the rhythms first before playing the piece. Although written as a solo, this piece could be played by dividing the different 'voices' between two or three guitars.

— a dot above or below a note means the note is to be played **staccato** (a short, detached note): damp the string with the fingers or thumb immediately after playing.

# Sweet Potato

Debbie Cracknell

# Moving from 1st to 2nd Position

The next four pieces use both 1st and 2nd positions. Move your hand up to 2nd position when you see the sign II. Be sure to move your thumb up the back of the neck of the guitar – do not 'leave it behind' when changing position. Keep the left hand square to the fingerboard.

## Gaelic Melody

Debbie Cracknell

## Jade

Debbie Cracknell

# In Corfu Town

Duet

Debbie Cracknell

# Allegro

Clementi
(1752—1832)

\*$\frac{3}{8}$ = Three quaver beats in a bar      \*♪ = semiquaver rest

# Two New Bass Accidentals

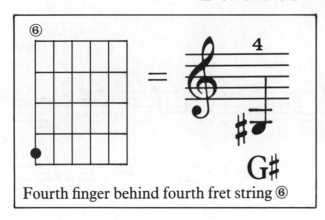

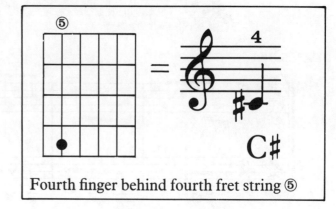

## Ragtime

# Test

Finger the following passage in *second* position:

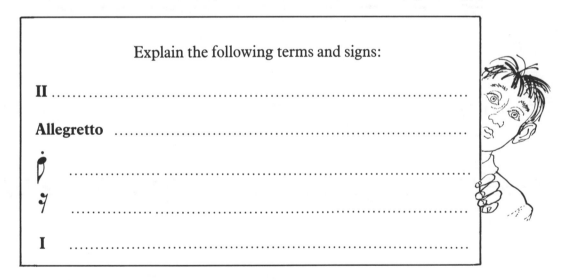

Explain the following terms and signs:

**II** ...............................................................................................

**Allegretto** ......................................................................................

͓ ......................................................................................

𝄾 ......................................................................................

**I** ......................................................................................

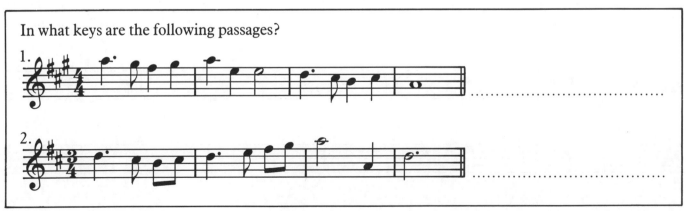

In what keys are the following passages?

1. ......................................................................

2. ......................................................................

# Slurs

A slur is a method of connecting two different notes together by playing the second note with the left hand to produce a smooth join.

## Upward Slurs

When slurring to a higher note, the second note is played by using the left hand finger as a hammer and hitting the string just behind the fret with the tip of the finger.

Play B with the right hand and then play C using the left hand finger as a hammer:

Now try C to D keeping C down as you hit D:

Exercises

# Danish Round

Play as a round. The second guitar starts
from the beginning when the first guitar
reaches the star.

# John Peel

English traditional

*  C = common time —
another way of writing $\frac{4}{4}$

# Shepherd's Song

Debbie Cracknell

# Downward Slurs

When moving from one note to a *lower* note, the left hand sounds the second note by pulling sideways (not upwards) off the string with the very tip of the finger. Keep the left hand square with the neck of the guitar; do not twist the hand away from the neck.

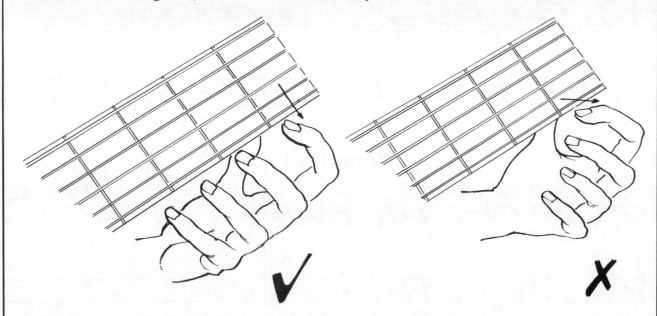

**Exercise 1**

When moving to another fingered note, hold the second note very firmly to make it sound clearly.

**Exercise 2**

# Waltz

Duet

Sor
(1778 – 1839)

* E♭ fingered as D♯ – string ④ fret 1

# Jam on the Freeway

**12/8** = Twelve quaver beats in a bar

Debbie Cracknell

to Coda

ponti.

*D.C. al ⊕ Coda

* nat.

ponti.

* *D.C. al ⊕* = repeat to the sign and then play the Coda (Italian for tail)

* nat. = play normally, i.e. not ponticello

# The Dotted Quaver

The dotted quaver ♪. works in the same way as the dotted crotchet. The dot makes the note half as long again: the dotted quaver is worth three quarters of a crotchet. It is often followed by a semiquaver to make up one crotchet beat

## Drone Tune

Debbie Cracknell

## Pastime with Good Company

16th-century

Some say that Henry VIII wrote the song 'Pastime with Good Company'. Henry was a musician, and the song certainly became a favourite at court.

# Moderato

A Trio using dotted quavers

Diabelli

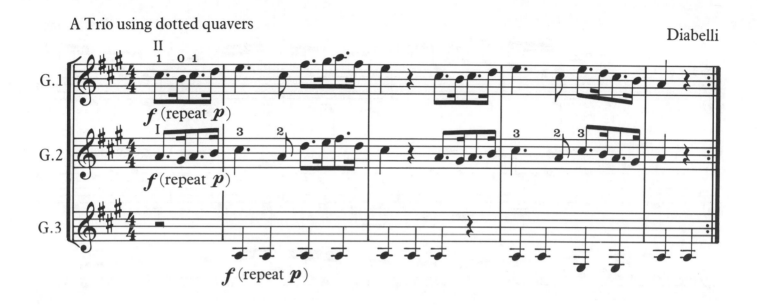

# Shaker Melody

Traditional

'St Patrick's Day' uses
the dotted quaver with a
**6/8** time signature.

# St Patrick's Day

Irish traditional

Count    1 2 & 3 4 5 6

'Los Gitanos' is not as difficult as it looks if these chords are practised first.

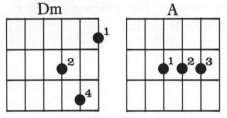

# Los Gitanos

Debbie Cracknell

*ad lib.* = take these passages in a free and easy manner — do not be too strict about keeping to the exact time.

i m a = strum these chords with the R.H. fingers in the direction of the arrows.

ras. (rasgueado) = strum across the strings with the backs of the R.H. fingers one after the other, beginning with the little finger (e): e − a − m − i.

# Sliding to the Third Position

The slide from the first to third position is often found in music which needs

D and B played together as a chord, or arpeggio.

The B can be found on string ③ fret 4, and this enables the D to be played with the B as a chord, or rapidly alternating with it in arpeggio style.

Exercises for sliding to third position

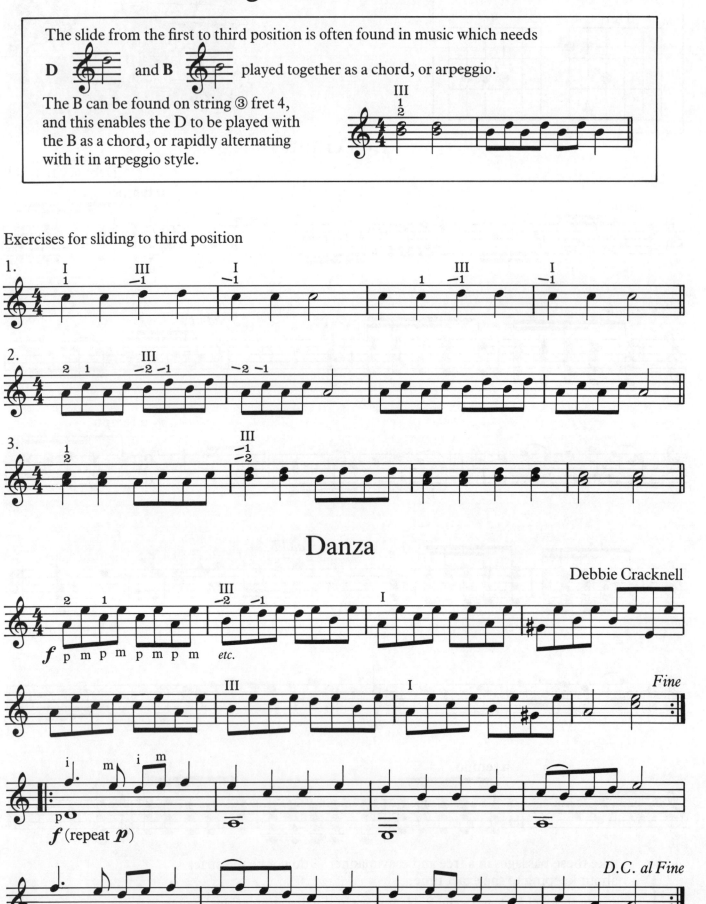

## Danza

Debbie Cracknell

# Andante

Debbie Cracknell

Dionisio Aguado was a Spanish guitarist and composer who was a friend of Fernando Sor (also Spanish) who composed the Waltz on page 25.

# Waltz

Aguado
(1784–1849)

\* take this G on string ④ fret 5

# The Fifth Position

The fifth position is a very common position on the guitar and many pieces require this move up the fingerboard.

When playing in the fifth position (indicated by V above the music) move your hand up the fingerboard so that —

finger 1 plays all the notes on the 5th fret
finger 2 plays all the notes on the 6th fret
finger 3 plays all the notes on the 7th fret
finger 4 plays all the notes on the 8th fret

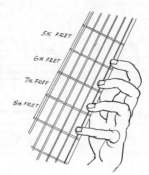

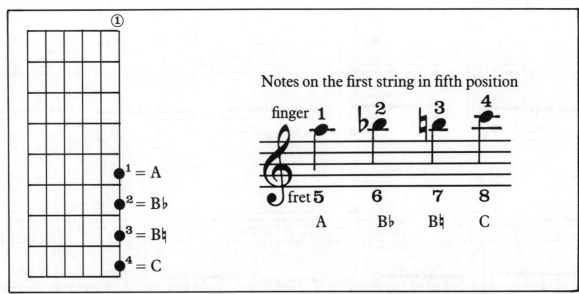

① 
$^1$ = A
$^2$ = B♭
$^3$ = B♮
$^4$ = C

Notes on the first string in fifth position

| finger | 1 | 2 | 3 | 4 |
|---|---|---|---|---|
| fret | 5 | 6 | 7 | 8 |
| | A | B♭ | B♮ | C |

Exercise 1

Exercise 2

# A Folly

Debbie Cracknell

# November

Duet version

Debbie Cracknell

**34**

In this more difficult solo version of 'November', note the change to a triplet quaver rhythm.

# November

Debbie Cracknell

\* This B can be taken on string ⑥ fret 7

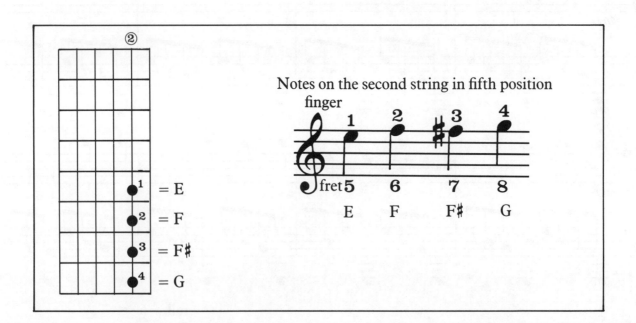

Notes on the second string in fifth position

① = E
② = F
③ = F♯
④ = G

Scale study using only 'natural' notes (no sharps or flats)

# Chorale

Debbie Cracknell

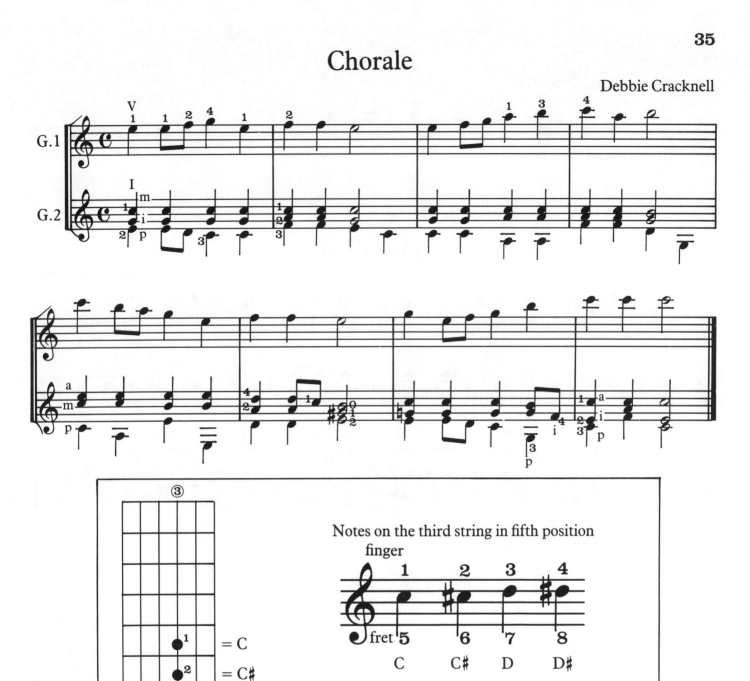

Notes on the third string in fifth position

# Finger aerobics!

After repeating each exercise two or three times try them on different strings.

Scale of C major in 5th position

Practise the C major scale before trying 'Jason's Jig'.

## Jason's Jig

Debbie Cracknell

\* **9/8** = nine quaver beats in a bar

Scale exercise in F major; B♭ in the key signature

The following three pieces are in the key of F major. Practise the scale exercise first to become used to the B♭.

## Cockles and Mussels

Irish traditional

# Plaisir D'Amour

French traditional

## When the Saints come marching in

American traditional

Trio

In 'Tricky Tango', guitar 1 is taken in the fifth position. This piece is in the key of G major (note the F♯ in the key signature). Practise guitars 1 & 2 together, and guitar 3 on its own before playing as an ensemble, as you will initially find the triplet rhythm difficult to play with the dotted quaver rhythm in the bass.

## Tricky Tango

Debbie Cracknell

# Oxford Blues

Debbie Cracknell

strum with m and a
rapidly up and down
first 3 strings

Guitar 1: try improvising on repeat, e.g.

*etc.*

# Test

Finger the following passage in *fifth* position:

V

Explain the following:

**3
8** ................................................

**ras.** ↟ ................................................

**III** ................................................

How many quavers in: ♪. .....................

How many quavers in: ♩ .....................

How many quavers in: ♩ .....................

How many semiquavers in: ♪. .....................

How many semiquavers in: ♩ .....................

How many semiquavers in: ♪ .....................

In what keys are the following passages?

Key ................

Key ................

# The Barré

Sometimes it is necessary to stop two or more strings at the same time with the index finger flat across the fingerboard, and this is called a **Barré**. Any number of strings from 2−5 is referred to as a half barré and will be indicated by the sign ½C or ₵. (Ceja is the Spanish term for barré.) When all six strings are stopped by the index finger it is known as a full barré and will be shown as C above the stave.

The barré sign is usually followed by a roman numeral to indicate the fret where it is to be taken.

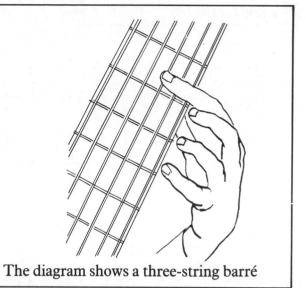

The diagram shows a three-string barré

The following four pieces use two- and three-string barrés.

## Aria

Debbie Cracknell

42

An anonymous Elizabethan
melody, originally written as
a solo for the lute.

# Packington's Pound

arranged by Debbie Cracknell

Try a different 'colour' (ponti., tasto) or
a change in volume $f$, $p$ etc. for the
repeats.

# Boulevard Barré

Debbie Cracknell

Repeat the last line *ad lib.* and gradually fade away.

Now try improvising with the half barré up and down the guitar fingerboard.

# A Reflection

Debbie Cracknell

# Three Repertoire Pieces
## with Study Notes

> Ferdinando Carulli was an Italian guitarist and composer who wrote around 400 works for the guitar, both solos and ensemble pieces.
> In this Waltz, try to bring out the melody as indicated by the accent signs >. Hold the dotted crotchets in the bass for their full value of three quaver beats.

## Waltz

Ferdinando Carulli
(1770–1841)

# Scarborough Fair

Take this setting of the traditional folk-song 'Scarborough Fair' at a steady pace. Be careful to hold all the ties and long notes for their full value; note that the C in bar 6 is taken on string ③ fret 5.

English traditional  arr. D. Cracknell

½CV

Francisco Tárrega was a Spanish guitarist and composer who was the founder of many of the techniques in use today on the classical guitar, notably the raising of the left leg with a footstool to support the guitar, and the development of the rest stroke.

In this piece try to emphasise the notes on the first string to bring out the melody (a rest stroke with finger a whilst p, i, m use free stroke is the most effective method — practise on open strings first). Take care to hold on to the long bass notes for their full value.

A full barré is used in bar 13. Keep the finger as straight as possible and very near the fret.

Do not expect a good sound straight away — it will come with practice!

# Study in C

Tárrega
(1852 – 1909)

# Manuscript

Printed in England by Caligraving Limited Thetford Norfolk